HOW WOULD YOU SURVIVE AS AN
AMERICAN INDIAN?

Written by
Scott Steedman

Illustrated by
Mark Bergin

Created & Designed by
David Salariya

FRANKLIN WATTS
A Division of Grolier Publishing

NEW YORK • LONDON • HONG KONG • SYDNEY
DANBURY, CONNECTICUT

D0060695

David Salariya   *Director*

Penny Clarke   *Editor*

Dr John Huitson   *Consultant*

SCOTT STEEDMAN

grew up in Australia and Prince George,
a town in western Canada. He studied
natural history at the University of
British Columbia, Vancouver, and has
edited many books on science and
history for children.

MARK BERGIN

was born in Hastings, England, in
1961. He studied at Eastbourne
College of Art and has specialized in
historical reconstruction since
leaving art school in 1983. He lives
in England with his wife and family.

DAVID SALARIYA

was born in Dundee, Scotland, where he
studied illustration and printmaking. He
has illustrated a wide range of books on
botanical, historical and mythical
subjects. He has created and designed
many new series of books for publishers
worldwide. In 1989 he established the
Salariya Book Company. He lives in
Brighton, England, with his wife, the
illustrator Shirley Willis.

Library of Congress Cataloging-in-Publication Data

Steedman, Scott.
    How would you survive as an American Indian? / by Scott Steedman;
    created & designed by David Salariya.
    p. cm. - (How would you survive?)
    Includes index.
    Summary: Describes the everyday life and customs of various Plains
    Indian tribes during the eighteenth and nineteenth centuries in North
    America.
    ISBN 0-531-14383-X (lib. bdg.)   0-531-15309-6 (pbk.)
    1. Indians of North America — Great Plains — Social life and
    customs — Juvenile literature. [1. Indians of North America — Great
    Plains.] I. Salariya, David. II. Title III. Series.
    E78.G73S775 1995
    978'.00497– dc20   95-16974
                                                           CIP AC

First American Edition 1995 by FRANKLIN WATTS
A Division of Grolier Publishing
Sherman Turnpike
Danbury, CT 06816
First Paperback Edtion·1997

DR. JOHN HUITSON

was born in North Shields in 1930. He
studied at the University of Durham and
then became principal of Darlington
College of Education. He joined the
American Museum in Britain, in Bath, as
deputy director and director of
education. He retired in 1995.

CONTENTS

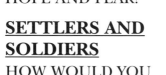

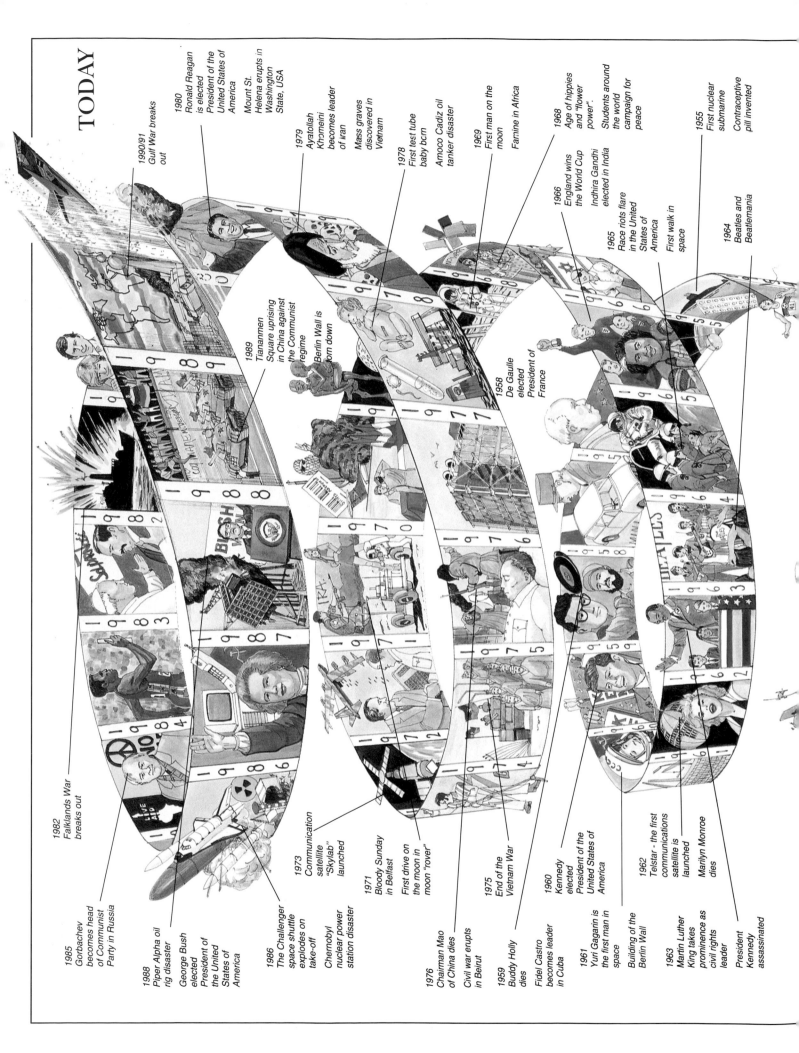

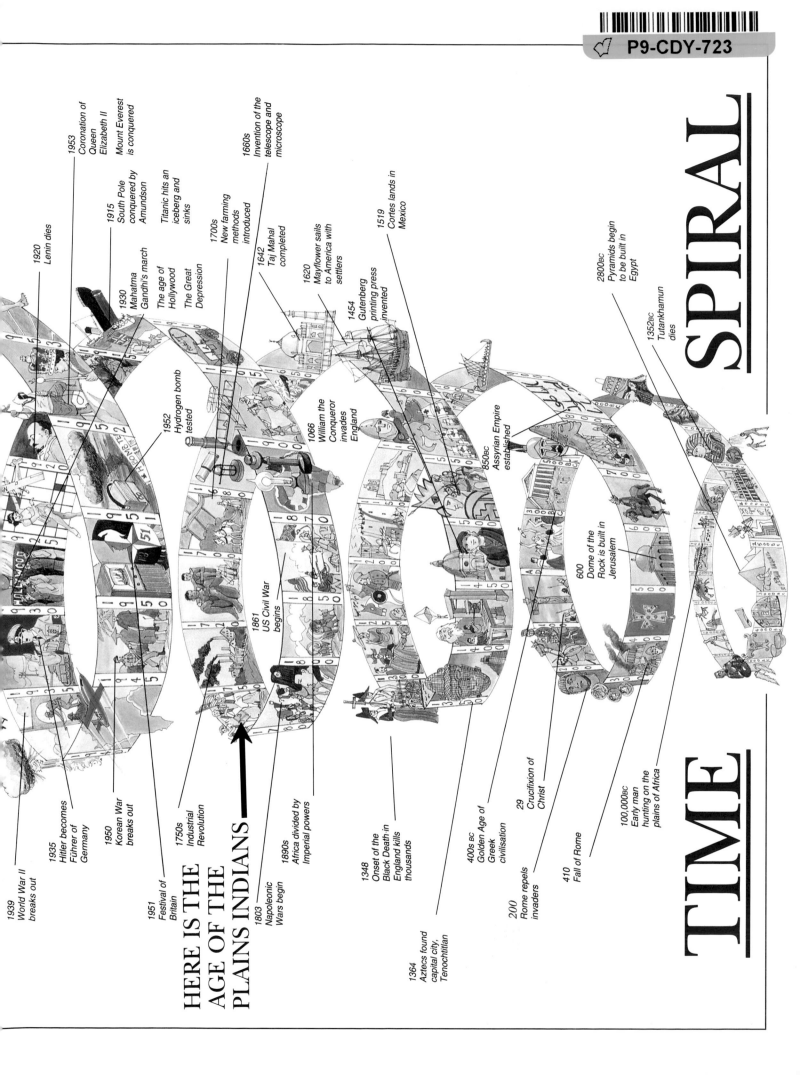

SPIRAL

TIME

HERE IS THE
AGE OF THE
PLAINS INDIANS

1939
World War II
breaks out

1935
Hitler becomes
Führer of
Germany

1950
Korean War
breaks out

1951
Festival of
Britain

1803
Napoleonic
Wars begin

1890s
Africa divided by
Imperial powers

1364
Aztecs found
capital city,
Tenochtitlan

1348
Onset of the
Black Death in
England kills
thousands

400s BC
Golden Age of
Greek
civilisation

200
Rome repels
invaders

29
Crucifixion of
Christ

410
Fall of Rome

100,000BC
Early man
hunting on the
plains of Africa

1920
Lenin dies

1953
Coronation of
Queen
Elizabeth II

Mount Everest
is conquered

1915
South Pole
conquered by
Amundsen

Titanic hits an
iceberg and
sinks

1930
Mahatma
Gandhi's march

The age of
Hollywood

The Great
Depression

1700s
New farming
methods
introduced

1660s
Invention of the
telescope and
microscope

1642
Taj Mahal
completed

1620
Mayflower sails
to America with
settlers

1454
Gutenberg
printing press
invented

1519
Cortes lands in
Mexico

2800BC
Pyramids begin
to be built in
Egypt

1352BC
Tutankhamun
dies

1952
Hydrogen bomb
tested

1066
William the
Conqueror
invades
England

850BC
Assyrian Empire
established

600
Dome of the
Rock is built in
Jerusalem

1861
US Civil War
begins

A Sea of Grass

YOU HAVE TRAVELED back in time to the age of the Plains Indians, from about A.D. 1700–1890. What do you see? In every direction the Great Plains of North America stretch out to the horizon. There are very few trees – just an endless sea of dry grass blowing in the wind. To the west, the grass is short and spindly; in the wetter east it may grow waist-high. Here and there, small hills or a river valley break the monotony of the flat landscape.

A Harsh Climate

THE PLAINS are a desolate place to live. All summer, the sun beats down from a cloudless sky, and temperatures often soar above 86°F (30°C). It hardly ever rains. Thunderstorms are common, but they are usually dry. The winters are long and bitterly cold, with temperatures regularly below minus 25°F (-3°C). In the wide expanse of land there is nothing to break the freezing wind. Snow blows across the windswept plains and piles up in the valleys and hollows.

Wild Animals

THE PLAINS ARE HOME to vast herds of buffalo, or bison. Several kinds of deer, including pronghorns, elk or wapiti, mule deer, and moose, are also common, as are grizzly bears, wolves, foxes, hares, rabbits, prairie dogs, porcupines, eagles, wild turkeys, and grouse. The few trees are cottonwoods, pines, or wild cherries. Wild turnips and herbs, such as sage, are common. In the dry west, cacti and camas flowers grow among the grass.

Food & Farming

THE PLAINS INDIANS' staple food is buffalo meat. If the big buffalo hunt in the summer is a success, the tribe will have enough meat for the long winter. Men also hunt elk, deer, rabbits, and grouse, and catch fish. There is very little farming on the vast and barren Plains. So women gather wild cherries, turnips, berries, and herbs. Some tribes grow tobacco, and those living in river valleys on the Plains eastern edge grow maize, beans, and squash.

A Nomadic Life

THE PLAINS INDIANS are nomads, or wanderers. Instead of living in permanent villages, they move camp with the seasons. Everything they have is portable: even their homes, tents called tepees, are easy to fold up and carry. In the summer, they follow the wandering herds of buffalo. Once a year, the bands come together for a great tribal gathering. Later they make their winter camp in a sheltered valley.

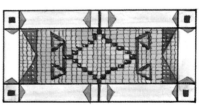

Crafts

UNLIKE OTHER INDIANS, the Plains people do not make many pots, rugs, or wooden carvings. These are all heavy and would weigh them down as they travel. But the women make beautiful clothes and jewelry and decorate them with embroidery, porcupine quills, and beads. Many men are also skilled artists. They mix their own pigments and paint scenes of battles or hunts on deer or buffalo skins, which they wear as robes or make into tepees.

BASIC FACTS ABOUT AMERICAN INDIAN LIFE

Gods & Spirits

THE INDIANS' WORLD is ruled by spirits, which are called Powers. The Powers flow through the sun, the moon, the earth, the sky, and every animal and plant on the Plains. People are careful to listen to the Powers, especially when they speak through dreams or visions. Medicine men can consult with the Powers and foretell the future or give people advice. The most powerful medicine men are great leaders. Some tribes, like the Sioux, believe in one chief Power, the Great Spirit.

Tribe, Band, Family

THERE ARE NEARLY 40 different tribes of Plains Indian. Each tribe speaks its own language and has its own ways and customs. A tribe is made up of several smaller groups called bands. The band members are usually all related to each other. You could count the number of families in a band by counting the tepees. Children live in their parents' tepee until they are married. Rich men can have several wives, but most are happy with one.

Hunting

HUNTING IS MAN'S WORK. The survival of the tribe depends on it, so boys are taught the skills at an early age. Before the white man introduced guns, the Indians killed buffalo with lances (spears), bows and arrows, or by driving them off cliffs onto the rocks below. The hunt is carefully planned. Scouts find the herd and drive it in the right direction. The hunters are superb riders, firing arrows or lancing a buffalo as they ride bareback through a stampeding herd.

Enemy Tribes

WARFARE IS A WAY OF LIFE. All the Plains tribes have traditional enemies whom they fight with great energy. The Sioux, for instance, hate the Pawnee. The tribes do not have armies or fight long campaigns. Instead, groups of warriors go on raids to steal horses, seek revenge, or prove their bravery. The greatest glory comes from counting *coup* – touching an enemy warrior. The leader of a successful raid is greatly respected, unless he loses men in battle.

Portable Homes

HOME IS A TEPEE, a large cone-shaped tent. It is made from buffalo hides that women have scraped clean and tanned. The hides are sewn together and then wrapped around a framework of long wooden poles. Inside there is a fire, the smoke escaping through a hole in the roof. There is almost always a bowl of soup or stew cooking, and anyone in the tribe can help themselves. At night the family sleeps on a layer of hides around the fire.

Communicating

IN THEIR YEARLY WANDERINGS, the Plains tribes are always meeting hunters or family groups from neighboring tribes. So how do they communicate? One way is by sign language, which all the tribes understand. Another way is by sending smoke signals, to tell a faraway group who they are, or if they have seen any buffalo. None of the tribes has a written language, so they record important events and legends with pictograms – pictures that tell a story.

Alaska

Northwest coast longhouse

Igloo

Inuit (Eskimo)

Tsimshian chiefs
in ceremonial costume

Birch-bark canoe

Hudson Bay

Grizzly bear

Eagle

Beaver

Rocky Mountains.

Wolf

Tepee

Missouri River

The Great Plains

Great Lakes

Blackfoot chief

Ute women

Buffalo (bison)

Mandan earth lodge

Comanche warrior

Wichita hunter

Cherokee man

Mandan: seminomadic tribes

Mississippi River

Tepee: nomadic tribes

Hopi dancer

IN THE LAST
ICE AGE, about
13,000 years
ago, a natural
land bridge
joined Alaska to
Siberia and
people walked
across from
Asia. These first
Americans
spread across
the vast
continent.

California

Gulf of Mexico

Mexico

North America (red) and the rest of the American continent

YOUR MAP OF THE INDIAN WORLD

THE BIG MAP shows North America as it was in A.D. 1492, the year that Christopher Columbus landed and European conquest of the continent began. There were more than 300 tribes of Native Americans spread across the vast continent, from the hot deserts of the south to the frozen tundra of the Arctic north. Columbus called them "Indios," because he thought he had reached the East Indies in Asia. Each tribe spoke its own language and lived by its own customs and traditions. Only the Aztecs of Mexico lived in big cities; most of the tribes of the north lived in small bands that survived by hunting or farming.

This book will focus on the Plains Indians, the tribes that lived on the Great Plains and prairies of central North America. These are the Indians made famous by cowboy movies, the ones who wore feather headdresses, smoked the peace pipe, lived in tepees, and went on the warpath. Their way of life was due to the horse. Introduced by Spanish settlers in the 1500s, it did not reach the Plains until the early 1700s. On horseback, Indians could travel great distances on raids or in search of the huge herds of buffalo that roamed the grasslands.

Labrador

Newfoundland

Iroquois warrior

Mohawk village

THE PEOPLE of the Northwest Coast lived in massive wooden longhouses and carved tall totem poles. The Inuit (Eskimo) of the Arctic hunted seals and whales. The tribes of the eastern woodlands made birch-bark canoes and lived in permanent villages surrounded by high wooden walls. The Plains tribes were nomads who followed the huge herds of buffalo. The Hopi and Zuni of the Southwest lived in pueblos, "apartment villages" made of mud bricks. The tribes of the Southeast were farmers and excellent weavers and potters.

THE PLAINS TRIBES spoke many different languages, but sign language helped them understand each other. Words were represented by hand movements.

THERE WERE more than forty tribes living on the Plains and prairies. The Plains tribes were true nomads. They hunted and lived in tepees all year. The prairie tribes were only nomads in the summer. When the cold weather came they returned to their villages and harvested the crops they had planted in the spring. All winter they lived in massive lodges made of earth and wood.

Florida

Moon When the Snow Drifts into the Tepees or Moon of Strong Cold (January)

Moon of the Snowblind (February) Geese-laying Moon (March)

Moon of the Red Grass Appearing (March/April)

WHAT ceremony is this crowd watching? *Go to pages 32-33*

HOW DO hunters catch this sacred bird? *Go to pages 38-39*

WHAT ARE dogs used for? *Go to pages 18-19*

HOW IS a tepee made? What is a tepee like inside? *Go to pages 14-15*

WHAT game are these boys playing? *Go to pages 30-31*

HERE AND ON the next two pages is a year in the life of a tribe of Plains Indians. Each page shows one season, from spring through to winter. It is not meant to be a true life picture, because you would never find all these things happening so close together, or at the same time. It is simply to act as your guide to this book. Start wherever you want and follow the Q options.

Moon When Ponies Shed (April/May)

Moon When Green Grass is (May/June)

Strawberry Moon or Summer Moon (June/July)

BEGIN YOUR NEW LIFE HERE

WHERE DO these wooden poles come from?
Go to pages 18-19

WHAT IS this man wearing?
Go to pages 26-27

WHY HAS this man painted his face?
Go to pages 32-33

HOW HAS this hunt been organized?
Go to pages 20-21

WHY HAS this hunter painted symbols on his horse?
Go to pages 36-37

WHAT WILL the Indians do with the dead buffalo?
Go to pages 22-23

WHAT other animals do the Plains Indians hunt?
Go to pages 20-21

 Moon When Chokecherries are Ripe (July/August)

 Moon When Geese Shed (August/September)

Drying Grass Moon (September/October)

WHAT ARE these buildings? Do the people live here all year? *Go to pages 14-15*

WHAT ARE these people doing? *Go to pages 22-23*

WHAT IS this drying in the sun? *Go to pages 24-25*

WHAT DOES the feather in this man's hair mean? *Go to pages 36-37*

DOES this man have two wives? *Go to pages 16-17*

WHAT crops are these women growing? What tools are they using? *Go to pages 24-25*

WHO IS the chief of this tribe? How was he elected? *Go to pages 34-35*

WHAT ARE his trousers made of? *Go to pages 26-27*

WHAT HAS this woman collected? *Go to pages 24-25*

WHO DID all the beadwork on this man's clothes? *Go to pages 28-29*

Moon of Falling Leaves (late October / November)

Moon of Popping Trees (November/ December)

Moon When Wolves Run Together (December)

HOW WILL this man hunt in the snow?
Go to pages 18-19

HOW MANY people live in each tepee?
Go to pages 16-17

IS THIS boy old enough to go hunting?
Go to pages 16-17

IS THIS a good time to go on the warpath?
Go to pages 36-37

WHY IS there a hole in the top of every tepee?
Go to pages 14-15

WHAT'S going on in this tepee?
Go to pages 30-31

AT HOME
WHERE WOULD YOU LIVE?

IF YOU WERE a Plains Indian, your home would be a tepee – a big, cone-shaped tent. All the members of the tribe, rich or poor, live in these portable homes. The tepee is built around a framework of long wooden poles. This is covered with several tanned buffalo hides sewn together into a single sheet. A fire always burns inside the tepee, at the very center. Two extra poles on the outside create a smoke hole at the top. In bad weather, these poles are brought together to keep rain or snow from getting in.

You and your whole family share the same tepee. There are no beds or chairs. The floor is covered with several layers of furs, where everyone, including the dogs, will curl up to sleep at night. Wooden spoons, pipes, skin bags, rawhide containers, and medicine bundles hang from the walls. All the cooking is done over the fire in the center. The entrance, covered with a round flap of buffalo hide, faces east toward the rising sun. The head of the family usually sits in the place of honor facing the door. Men often paint their tepee covers with scenes from great battles or hunts they have led or taken part in. But it is the women who always put up, look after, and take down the family tepee, and it really belongs to them.

The sweat lodge is used by men to sweat, meditate, and be ceremonially purified. It is made of willow saplings covered with skins. Water thrown on the fire turns to steam.

This is the way the Cheyenne tribe organize their tepees during their yearly get-together. The five bands camp together in a big circle. In the center is the large council tepee.

The tepee cover is made of as many as 22 buffalo skins sewn in a semi-circle. The "ears" at the top are smoke flaps.

Some tribes build their tepees around three main poles; others use four. These are lashed together with rope.

The main poles are set up in a circle and many other lighter poles are added. An average tepee has 20 to 30 poles.

The skin cover is wrapped around the frame and held together with wooden pins. Then the entrance flap and the smoke hole poles are added.

Q

You need to pack up the family tepee and load it onto a horse. How do you do this?
Go to pages 18-19

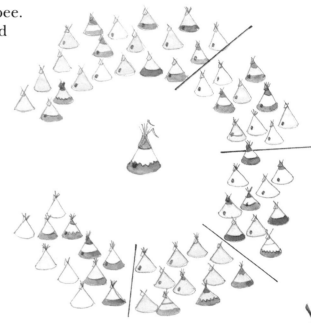

a

b

c

d

Some of the things you might find inside a tepee.
a A fringed rawhide bag where a man stores important ceremonial items.
b A backrest. The

Blackfoot and Crow tribes use these.
c Sioux tepee ornament, made of quillwork.
d Sewing kits include bone or antler needles.

Tribes from the edges of the Plains do not all live in tepees. The Sauk and Fox

people make dome-shaped lodges covered with large pieces of bark.

Some tribes from the northern Plains, such as the Chippewa, make tepees with

bark. Twigs hold the bark in place. These tepees are also known as wigwams.

In the winter the Wichita tribe of the southern Plains lives in dome-shaped

houses thatched with grass. In the hot summer months they use tepees.

The Pawnee and Mandan spend the winter in lodges. These are much bigger and stronger than tepees. They are made of heavy logs covered with hard-packed dirt. The lodge is circular, with a curved roof and a covered entrance. Forty or more people and their animals live inside.

The tepee is small, so there are rules to avoid arguments. Every member of the family has his or her place to sit. Dogs and people come and go all the time. It is rude to walk between another person and the fire. If you want to pass, let them know, and they will lean forward and let you walk behind them.

Top view showing stones holding down the tepee cover.

Outside the tepee a man might erect a frame to hold his shield and medicine bundle.

YOUR FAMILY
WHO WOULD LIVE WITH YOU?

Parents usually arrange marriages for their children. But they are flexible, and some couples marry for love.

If a boy and girl are in love, their parents may let them pick berries together. Or they can talk outside her tepee.

Sometimes a boy and girl are not allowed to speak. So he sends her coded messages by playing his flute by her tepee.

The wedding ceremony is simple. The groom's family give the bride's family gifts of horses, blankets, and buffalo skins.

Q

How do you learn to prepare skins for your future husband?
Go to page 22

There are 14 tepees with about 100 people in this band. The women are busy making clothes, preparing food, scraping buffalo hides, and putting buffalo meat out to dry. A group of men is discussing the value of a horse they stole in a raid.

A family's wealth is measured by how many horses they own. An important chief may have several hundred. In most tribes, men look after the horses. But Comanche women tend their own herds.

Tepee covers are rolled up in warm weather to let air in.

Children run to meet a hunting party that has returned with a deer.

AS A PLAINS INDIAN, you spend all year traveling and camping with your band. Almost everyone in the band is related: as brothers and sisters, aunts and uncles, nephews and nieces, or cousins. So it is like a huge extended family, and you know everyone well. There could be between 10 and 50 tepees in your band, with one family living in each tepee. Every band has a chief. It also has a nickname, such as the Hairy Band or Those Who Move Often. Now and then you meet other bands in your tribe, and you may camp or hunt together for a while. Once a year, in the early summer, all the bands come together at a special spot for a huge tribal gathering.

You are lucky, the Indians love children, so if you get into mischief you won't be smacked or disciplined. You'll also spend most of your time

HUSBANDS & WIVES

A good wife gathers firewood and water, collects berries and herbs, and takes care of the children. She is good at crafts and keeps a clean tepee.

A man is judged by his horsemanship and his skill as a hunter and warrior. He is expected to provide meat for the family and do heavy work.

Most men have one wife, but rich men can have as many as four or five. Women can have only one husband. Either partner can end the marriage without fuss.

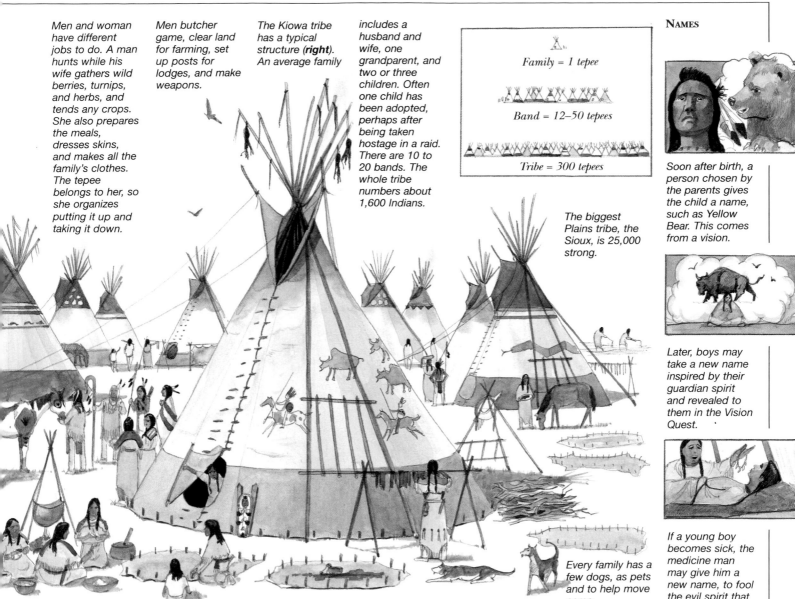

Men and woman have different jobs to do. A man hunts while his wife gathers wild berries, turnips, and herbs, and tends any crops. She also prepares the meals, dresses skins, and makes all the family's clothes. The tepee belongs to her, so she organizes putting it up and taking it down.

Men butcher game, clear land for farming, set up posts for lodges, and make weapons.

The Kiowa tribe has a typical structure (**right**). An average family includes a husband and wife, one grandparent, and two or three children. Often one child has been adopted, perhaps after being taken hostage in a raid. There are 10 to 20 bands. The whole tribe numbers about 1,600 Indians.

Family = 1 tepee

Band = 12–50 tepees

Tribe = 300 tepees

The biggest Plains tribe, the Sioux, is 25,000 strong.

Every family has a few dogs, as pets and to help move camp.

NAMES

Soon after birth, a person chosen by the parents gives the child a name, such as Yellow Bear. This comes from a vision.

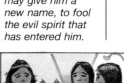

Later, boys may take a new name inspired by their guardian spirit and revealed to them in the Vision Quest.

If a young boy becomes sick, the medicine man may give him a new name, to fool the evil spirit that has entered him.

Often a person is given a nickname, such as Scared of Snakes, because of something remarkable he or she has done.

playing. There are no schools, so you'll learn everything you need to know by copying your parents and older relatives. You'll start riding when you're age four or five, and will be really skilled by the time you're seven. If you're a boy you'll learn to hunt with little bows and arrows, while your sister plays house with miniature tepees.

As a girl, when you come of age, you will be separated from the band. Alone with your mother, you'll learn traditional skills like painting, beadwork, and porcupine-quill embroidery. A boy becomes a man by undertaking a Vision Quest. You will go off on your own and wait for your personal guardian spirit to come to you. Afterward you'll assemble your own medicine bundle to help you in battle. Now you will be able to go on raids and help your father hunt.

BIRTH
A woman gives birth in her tepee, with the help of a midwife. The baby is dried with

dry wood shavings or moss and placed in a hide bag stuffed with moss.

Every child is given a second set of parents, like godparents. They look after

the child if the real parents are away, and adopt him or her if the parents die.

Many children die of accidents or disease. If their child is killed, a family will often

adopt a child who has been taken in a raid or one who has no parents.

Q

You are a boy, and old enough to make a Vision Quest. What should you do?
Go to page 38

ON THE MOVE
WHAT WAS TRAVELING LIKE?

The first step in making a dugout canoe is felling a large tree. This is done with a stone-headed ax.

Burning coals are placed on the log and the burned wood is scraped away. The log is gradually hollowed out.

Lighter canoes are made with large pieces of birch bark. These are cut from birch trees in thick sheets.

The shell is made by sewing the pieces of bark together with roots. A wooden frame is added. All joints are sealed with spruce gum.

Q

Your family goes collecting wild rice in their canoe. How can you help?
Go to page 25

Young men with lances watch the valley below.

The medicine man leads the way as this tribe moves camp.

I T IS TIME TO MOVE CAMP. The women pack up the tepees, using the poles to make special carrying frames called travois. They wrap up all the family's belongings in hides and the tepee cover and load these onto travois, which are pulled by horses and dogs. The men guard the convoy, their weapons at the ready. Scouts ride ahead and fan out in all directions, scanning the horizon for enemies. Sometimes the medicine man heads the convoy, otherwise the richest families lead the way. They may have as many as 70 to 100 horses, some dragging travois, the others running free. Ordinary families with 5 or 6 horses each come next. At the rear are more scouts and the poorest families, walking or riding borrowed horses. On a good day the band covers 12 miles (20 km).

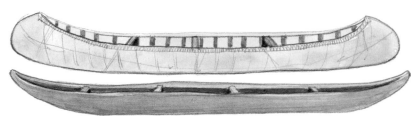

The tribes on the edges of the Plains travel by canoe, using the many rivers as highways. Dugout canoes (**bottom**) are stronger than bark craft. But they are also heavier and harder to carry around rapids or between river systems. The Chippewa hunt and pick wild rice from birch-bark canoes (**top**). The Hidatsa paddle across the Missouri River in bull boats made of buffalo hides stretched across a wooden frame. These are light enough to be carried on the back with a strap.

LIKE TEPEES, travois are usually made and owned by women. The poles are lashed together with rawhide. The band sticks to high ground, where the view is best and the grass is short. Tall grass makes traveling harder.

Unlike other horse people, such as the Mongols, the Plains tribes do not milk their horses and only eat horse meat if they are starving.

HUNTING & HEAVY LOADS

In winter, when snow covers the ground in deep drifts, hunters wear snowshoes to stalk buffalo, moose, and deer.

The snowshoes are made of rawhide webbing stretched over a wooden frame. They are nearly 6½ feet (2 m) long.

A strong horse can drag a load of 265 pounds (120 kg) on a travois.

Babies travel in cradleboards that their mothers sling from their saddles as they ride.

Children run along beside the horses. When they get tired, they hitch a ride on one of the family's travois.

Before they had horses, men and women carried heavy loads on their backs. First the items were rolled up in a

Horses, which reached the Plains in the early 1700s, completely transformed Indian life. The Plains tribes bought or stole horses from neighboring tribes, who had obtained them from Spanish settlements in what is now New Mexico. The Plains Indians soon became superb horsemen. The greatest riders of all, the Comanche, call horses "sacred dogs." On horseback, the Indians can travel great distances across the Plains on hunts or raids. They make their own saddles from animal hide stuffed with grass. Horses run wild, and men run them down, lasso them, and break them in. A man often ties his favorite horse to his tepee peg, where enemy raiders would find it harder to steal.

pack. (The pack was tied tight.) Then it was carried with the aid of a "burden band," a strap across the forehead.

TRANSPORT

This Blackfoot carrying pouch is decorated with colorful beadwork.

Before the coming of the horse, dogs and women dragged the heavy travois.

Now women can ride. But the Indians still make their dogs pull small travois.

The horse travois is much bigger. The poles can be 16 or 20 feet (5 or 6 m) long.

Small loads can also be tied onto a dog's back.

Q

Your family is poor. The chief offers you two blankets and some buffalo meat. Should you be insulted? *Go to pages 34-35*

THE BUFFALO HUNT

HOW WOULD YOU HELP IN THE HUNT?

The arrival of the buffalo herds is a time of great excitement. Many tribes hold dances to bring the buffalo to them.

Buffalo have poor eyesight but an excellent sense of smell. Hunters creep up on them from downwind.

Accidents are common. Riders fall and are pummeled by the herd. Hunters are gored by wounded buffalo.

The hunters respect the buffalo. A man who kills a bull eats its heart to share in its strength and bravery.

Q

What will you do with the buffalo's internal organs? *Go to pages 22-23*

IN THE SUMMER, the buffalo gather on the Plains in huge herds thousands strong. The grass is hidden by a heaving sea of dark hides and the ground rumbles with the herd's hoof beats.

Mounted on their fastest, most agile horses, these Indians run down a group of buffalo and kill as many as they can. The hunters must be fearless riders, because the buffalo are fast and strong, and firing from the saddle is very difficult. Another way of hunting is to surround the herd so the animals mill around in confusion. Then hunters pick off the buffalo one by one.

The whole of your tribe gathers for the yearly hunt. Scouts go out to find the herds, and everyone is busy making weapons. As soon as a herd is spotted, the hunting party mounts their best "buffalo horses" and set off. The hunt is strictly organized and everyone has a role to play. Warriors keep guard for enemy Indians, and "police" keep order to make sure no one frightens the buffalo. The hunters approach the herd in a line, then charge into the middle with whoops and yells. In the wild chase that follows, each hunter singles out an animal and kills it with his lance, bow and arrow, or, after the 1860s, his rifle.

Buffalo are not afraid of wolves and allow them to approach the herd. So one or

two hunters dress up in wolf hides and creep up on small groups of buffalo.

From the earliest times, Indians hunted buffalo by driving them over cliffs. They used

Head-Smashed-In Buffalo Jump in Alberta, Canada, for nearly 6,000 years.

Another method is to start a grass fire on three sides of the herd. In their panic the

buffalo run toward the gap in the ring of fire, where hunters lie in ambush.

Before the introduction of repeating rifles in the 1860s, the Indians hunted buffalo with bows and arrows and lances. A hunter could kill a buffalo with one or two well-placed arrows.

The rare white buffalo is sacred. The arrows that killed it and the knife used to cut it up are purified in sweetgrass smoke.

OTHER QUARRY

The biggest members of the deer family, moose have huge antlers. They are hunted on the northern Plains.

After the buffalo, the most important prey is the pronghorn antelope. The elk is larger, but less common.

Beaver furs are traded with whites, who value them because of the European fashion for fur hats.

Eagles are sacred birds caught for their beautiful feathers. Only men with special powers can hunt them.

Hunting weapons. **a** The Sharps rifle can kill a buffalo from a mile away.

b Bow cover and quiver. **c** Arrows are about 2 feet (60 cm) long, made of service-berry, currant, or dogwood with split hawk feathers at one end, and stone or metal tips. **d** Bows are made of wood or elk or bighorn sheep antler. The string is a sinew.

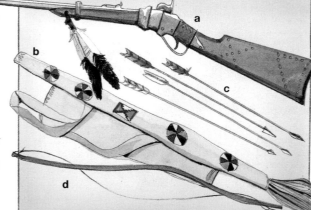

During the annual hunt, the element of surprise is very important. No one is allowed to hunt on their own in case they scare off the herd. If anyone is caught doing this, he is flogged, his weapons are broken, or his tepee may be burned. Each hunter puts distinctive marks on the shafts of his arrows, so the buffalo he kills can be identified.

In the winter, men of the Arapaho and Assiniboin tribes hunt buffalo on snowshoes. The animals get stuck in the deep snow and are easy to kill.

As soon as the men set out on a hunting party, the women pack up camp and follow. Messengers ride back to tell them how the hunt has gone.

A successful hunt is cause for celebration. The tribe holds a feast and everyone eats their fill of buffalo meat. Hunters tell stories of their exploits.

Q

You need some eagle feathers for a headdress. How will you get them?
Go to pages 38-39

AFTER THE HUNT

HOW WOULD YOU USE THE DEAD BUFFALO?

Men, women, and children skin the dead buffalo where they have fallen. A big animal weighs a ton, so it takes several men to move it into the right position. Then the skin is cut away with knives made of bone or sharp stones such as flint.

Back at the camp, your mother stretches out the hide, hair side down, and stakes it with wooden pegs. Then she uses a tooth-edged tool made from bone or horn to scrape away all the blood, fat, muscle, and connective tissue.

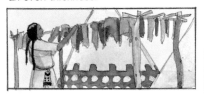

Next she turns the hide over and scrapes off the hair with an adze-shaped tool made of antler. If she is going to make a warm hat or robe, she will leave the hair on. Then she scrapes the hide again with the adze until it is an even thickness.

The hot summers of the Plains are excellent for drying buffalo meat. Your mother hangs long strips on wooden frames to dry in the open.

Moose or deer hides are thrown over a log and scraped with tools made from rib or leg bones.

A LMOST EVERYTHING YOU AND YOUR FAMILY own or need is made from the buffalo. Every part of the dead animal is used. As soon as the hunt is over, all the women and children join the men skinning the dead buffalo and cutting up the meat. A big buffalo gives 1,100 to 1,320 pounds (500 to 600 kg). Tender morsels such as the liver and the kidneys are eaten right away. The tongue is thought to be a great delicacy. Once it is cut up the buffalo can be loaded onto horses and carried back to camp.

Your mother and aunts join the other women in the painstaking work of preparing the buffalo hides. If the hide is to be used to make a tepee cover, they lie the buffalo on its back and remove the hide in one piece. To make a robe, they skin the animal on its stomach, making a long cut down the backbone from the head to the tail. Then they stake out the hide and remove all the flesh and hair with special scrapers. The rawhide may then be tanned to make leather.

The meat is cut into strips and hung up to dry. It is later mixed with fat and wild cherries to make pemmican, a high-protein food that will feed the tribe for many months.

Items made from buffalo:
a *Horn cup*
b *Horn ladle*
c *Gunpowder flask*
d *Winter gloves*
e *Painted skull used in the Sun Dance*
f *Rope made from buffalo hair*

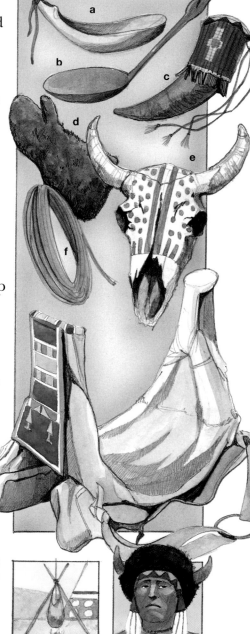

Women's saddles have high pommels. The wooden frame is covered with stretched rawhide.

Men's saddles are lower, with no frame.

Q

Your uncle has saved a buffalo skull for next year's Sun Dance. What will happen?
Go to pages 32-33

MAKING LEATHER

The first step in preparing leather is to make a mixture of fat and buffalo brains. This is rubbed into the hide, which is then left to dry in the sun.

Then the skin is rubbed through a loop of sinew to dry and soften it.

Finally the skin is smoked on a wooden framework set up over a fire.

The stomach and bladder can be hung over a fire and used as cooking pots.

Men in certain secret societies wear headdresses with buffalo horns.

Tanned hides are used to make tepee covers, blankets (**b**), belts, moccasin uppers (**a**), leggings, dresses, caps, mittens, pouches, gun cases, dolls, and lassos. Buffalo horns are made into spoons, cups, ladles, powder flasks, fire carriers, toys, and rattles. The hair is made into ropes, halters, brushes, and head-dresses, and used as stuffing for pillows and saddles.

The Indians make their clothes from raw or tanned hide. Rawhide is also used to make containers (**d**), such as trunks for storage or parfleches (square bags) for carrying food (**c**), saddles, buckets, ropes, knife sheaths, rattles, shields (**g**), drums, bridles, bull boats, masks, thonging for snowshoes and travois, and protective covers (**e**) for quivers, and lances (**f**).

j

The bones are used for knives, hoes, shovels, and scrapers for preparing hides (**j**), game counters, skate blades, and sled runners. The tongue, heart, liver, kidneys, brains, and bone marrow are eaten and the fresh blood drunk.

k

The hooves are turned into rattles (**i**) or melted down to make glue, kept in wooden bowls (**k**). Sinews provide bow strings, grips, and sewing thread. The tail is dried and used as a medicine switch (**h**), fly swatter or riding whip. It could also be used to decorate a tepee or is put in a medicine bundle.

l

The stomach and bladder are covered in leather to make water carriers (**l**). The women gather dry buffalo dung and burn it as a fuel. The men also smoke it in special ceremonies.

Q

On a hunting trip, you kill a white buffalo, a sacred animal. What should you do?
Go to page 21

MEALTIME
WHAT WOULD YOU EAT AND DRINK?

The fire drill is rubbed vigorously between the palms until the tinder – bark or buffalo droppings – catches fire.

Water is boiled in a buffalo paunch. Hot stones are lifted out of the fire and dropped into the skin receptacle.

Meat is roasted on a stick balanced over the fire. It could also be boiled in a pot or grilled over the hot coals.

A few tribes, including the Blackfoot from the northern Plains, make earthenware cooking pots.

Q

Your uncle asks you to go with him to the sacred quarry where the red stone for making pipes is found. Will it be safe?
Go to page 28

This woman is cooking in a metal pot. It has been traded with tribes to the east, who got it from white traders.

In the heat of summer the tribes set up sun shelters.

The Plains tribes either grow tobacco or trade it from their neighbors. The men chew it or smoke it in pipes.

AS A PLAINS INDIAN YOU WILL LIVE ON MEAT, especially buffalo meat. The Blackfoot call buffalo flesh "real meat." But like all the Plains tribes, they also eat moose, deer, elk, rabbits, and fish. The best meat is roasted or grilled fresh. But game cannot be found every day, and the buffalo herds may disappear for months at a time. That is why your mother and the other women dry so much meat after each hunt.

The men do all the hunting, but women gather wild plant foods and cook all the meals. From an early age your sister and the other girls learn to find wild cherries, berries, strawberries, plums, and herbs such as sage. The wild Prairie turnip, with its fat, deep root, is dug up in early summer, then peeled and dried to be eaten for the rest of the year. Your mother may bake some fresh turnips in the hot ashes of the fire.

In early spring, the Ojibwa tap maple trees and collect the sweet sap in wooden buckets.

They boil it down to make maple syrup and sugar, for sweetening a wide range of foods.

Wild cherries are used to sweeten other food as well as to make pemmican.

There are also many varieties of berries, such as Saskatoon or service berries.

Pemmican is made by crushing wild cherries, pits and all, with a stone maul. This paste is then mixed with sun-dried buffalo meat, melted fat, and bone marrow.

Buffalo meat is pounded flat with a heavy stone tool called a maul.

The wooden frame for drying meat is usually out beside the family tepee.

Most Plains Indians catch fish only when other food is scarce. The Cree catch them in weirs, while the Blackfoot use simple traps woven from willow saplings (**above**).

Women use bone tools to dig up wild turnips, which have deep roots.

In the winter, the Cree also spear fish through breaks they make in the river ice.

When they sow their maize, the Indians of the prairies often place a small fish in each hole. This acts as a fertilizer.

When men meet, they smoke together in silence before getting down to business. As the Sioux man Chased-By-Bears explained it, "Before talking of holy things . . . one will fill his pipe and hand it to the other, who will light it and offer it to the sky and earth . . . they will smoke together. . . . Then will they be ready to talk." While the men talk, their wives prepare food. This woman is pounding buffalo meat to make pemmican. Her daughter holds a rawhide sack full of berries she has just collected.

The ground is first broken up with hoes made from the shoulder blades of buffalo or elk. Then the maize is planted.

The hard work of harvesting the maize is done by women. If the crops are far from the village, men stand guard.

Blackfoot women use long sticks to dig up roots of the camas plant. They eat only the roots of the blue-flowered camas. The white-flowered sort is poisonous.

On the western Plains, women gather the roots of the camas flower. They bake these in deep pits lined with burning-hot stones and wet willow branches.

The seminomadic tribes like the Pawnee and Mandan also grow their own crops. The most important crop is maize, but squash, beans, and sunflowers are also cultivated. The true nomads, like the Sioux and the Comanche, grow no crops, but they eat some maize which they trade with their neighbors for skins or horses.

WILD RICE

The Eastern Sioux and Cree gather wild rice from canoes. A man paddles while his wife beats the rice. The seeds fall into the canoe.

Back in camp, the woman lays the kernels out to dry in the sun. Then she sets up a flat frame above a smoldering fire near her tepee and dries the rice kernels.

The rice is put in a hollow tree trunk and pounded to break open the husks.

Finally the rice is thrown in the air to separate the grain from the chaff.

Q

You need to make a new birch-bark canoe. How is it done?
Go to page 18

YOUR CLOTHES
WHAT WOULD YOU WEAR?

It takes the skin of two deer to make a man's shirt. Each skin is cut into three pieces as shown. The head is not used.

YOUR CLOTHES are made of buffalo and deerskin, often decorated with furs, feathers, fringes, and strips of ornamental beadwork. Your father and the other men wear quilled shirts and leggings reaching to the hip. Your mother and aunts wear long, sleeveless dresses of deer or soft mountain-sheep hide over knee-high leggings. On top of this, both men and women often wrap themselves in a simple buffalo robe. Everyone wears soft moccasins on their feet.

All the clothes are made by the women. They use a bone awl to punch holes in hides, and sew them with buffalo sinews.

Rubbing your hair with buffalo fat helps to keep it glossy. You brush it with the rough side of a buffalo's tongue. Your father shaves with shells. When you are old enough you may want a tattoo.

The front legs form the shirt's arms. The man's head pokes through where the deer's was, and the hind legs hang down his legs.

A woman's dress is also made from two deer skins. An extra piece is sewn across the shoulders.

Sioux men wear armbands made of hide and lengths of horsehair.

An eagle-feather warbonnet is the greatest trophy a warrior can claim. This one is Sioux. It is worn only in battle or at important ceremonies. The feathers are tipped with horsehair.

Sioux moccasin decorated with geometric patterns. Each shape has a name.

Sioux warrior's breastplate made with bird bones.

Q

On your first raid you kill an enemy and take his scalp. What sort of feather should you wear in your hair?
Go to page 37

HAIRSTYLES & HEADDRESSES

This Kiowa woman parts her hair in the middle. She may paint the part red.

This Blackfoot woman's head-dress shows she belongs to a secret society.

An elderly Blackfoot woman keeps her loose hair in place with a head cloth.

A Crow warrior wears an eagle hairpiece on the crown of his head.

This Blackfoot man has braids, a cropped crown, and fore-head lock.

Pawnee men shave their heads, leaving a closely-cropped central strip.

All Indians wear jewelry. But only great warriors or leaders can wear grizzly bear claw necklaces.

The decorations on an Indian's clothes have special meanings. This man is wearing a loose deerskin shirt painted with horses and birds. These animals have great symbolic power and may represent the man's brave deeds, or spirits revealed to him in a vision. The leader of a raid may put on a wolf robe or wrap himself in the skin of an eagle, to take on the power of a beast of prey.

MAKING MOCCASINS

These skin shoes are worn by all Plains Indians. This is a Sioux pattern for a two-piece pair.

The sole is made of hard-wearing rawhide. The upper is softer tanned hide, and the lace is a thin leather thong.

Moccasins can also be made from a single piece of tanned leather. This is a Blackfoot one-piece pattern.

Unlike the Sioux moccasin, this shoe has a tongue. Both pairs are decorated with beadwork.

Q
Your parents are both killed in an attack by Pawnee raiders. What will become of you?
Go to page 17

Babies are wrapped in a skin and strapped into a cradleboard, which the mother wears like a backpack. The covers may be richly decorated with quillwork.

The colors of decoration are symbolic: red means sunset or thunder; yellow the dawn or the earth; blue the sky or day; black the night; green the summer.

Girls soon copy their mothers. They often dress up a puppy or doll and carry it in a cradle like a baby. Their ears are pierced in public ceremonies.

Sacred pipes are made from hard stone, especially red catlinite. The only quarry is on Sioux land, in Minnesota.

The quarry is a very holy place, and other tribes may come in peace to chisel pipes from the rock.

The rough-hewn shape is rounded and smoothed by rubbing with a hard stone tool. This is very slow.

The smoke holes are hollowed out. Lastly, shallow geometric decorations are carved onto the pipe's surface.

ARTS & CRAFTS
WHAT WOULD YOU MAKE?

CLOTHES, TEPEES, BLANKETS, even horses – everything is brightened with beautiful painting and beadwork.

Women adorn leather clothes and objects, adding fringes and sewing on feathers, horsehair, or elk teeth. They excel at porcupine-quill embroidery. The men kill these cat-sized animals and pluck out their sharp spines. Then the women sort the quills by size, using the largest ones for everyday bags and saving the finest hairs to decorate important objects. As she works, the woman sucks each quill gently to soften it, then flattens it with her fingernail. She may dye the quills before sewing them into place.

Plains arts and crafts were transformed by the new materials brought by white people. Embroidery is a good example. Colorful glass beads replaced porcupine quills. But the traditional skills and patterns flourished, and women produced beautiful beadwork.

The Blackfoot believe that their pipe is a gift of the Power (spirit) of thunder.

This Sioux, or Iowa, pipe is carved with a dog and a white man, identified by his flat hat.

Men and horses are common on robes. Buffalo are rare and dogs are never shown.

Man in a robe painted with battle scenes. The shapes represent mounted warriors and personal spirits.

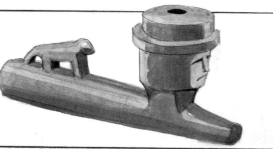

PICTOGRAMS

Q
You have just been married, and need to make a tepee of your own. How is it done?
Go to page 14

The first step in painting a pictogram is to stake the buffalo hide.

The colors red, brown, and yellow come from clays, black from charcoal or dark earth.

He grinds up the colors in a stone mortar, adding a glue made from buffalo hooves.

Each color is kept in a shell or hollow stone. The man presses his design on the hide.

Then he paints it in with brushes made of antelope hair or tools of bone or wood.

The finished work is set with a layer of glue, again made from the hooves of buffalo.

A man painting a buffalo hide with scenes of his battles. In one he kills an enemy with a lance; in others he scalps two women and "counts coup." He also fires at an enemy war party, and revenges his brother's murder.

A Sioux woman embroiders a saddlebag with geometric bead-work patterns. Behind her is a buckskin dress she has just decorated. Beadwork is slow, but it is faster than the old porcupine-quill embroidery. The thread is buffalo sinews and the needles are made of bone or antler.

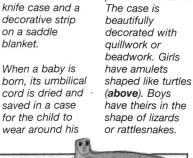

(**Top**) Closeup of beadwork on a knife case and a decorative strip on a saddle blanket.

When a baby is born, its umbilical cord is dried and saved in a case for the child to wear around his or her neck as a protective charm. The case is beautifully decorated with quillwork or beadwork. Girls have amulets shaped like turtles (**above**). Boys have theirs in the shape of lizards or rattlesnakes.

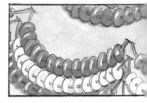

BEADWORK STITCHING

Lazy stitch is used for simple geometric patterns. Several rows of beads are sewn at each end and pulled tight.

In Crow stitch, rows of different colored beads are fastened at right angles. The result is still strictly linear.

Freer curving patterns are made with Netted stitch. The beads are held down with criss-crossing threads.

The edge of the leather object is decorated with a single row of beads using a simple looping stitch.

Q

A scout rides into camp shouting that he has seen a herd of buffalo. What will happen now?
Go to pages 20-21

For thousands of years Indians have made tools and weapons from hard stones

such as flint. By chipping away at the flint they make tools and spearheads.

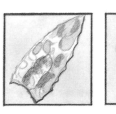

Wood and wood carving are both rare on the Plains. This is a Sioux coup stick.

The heavy ends of wooden warclubs are often carved like people's heads.

Spoons and bowls are carved from burls – hard knots of wood. These Sioux feast bowls are made of ash (**left**) and maple (**right**). They are thin and light but strong.

GAMES AND STORIES
HOW WOULD YOU HAVE FUN?

WHEN THE HUNTING IS GOOD, you and the rest of your band have plenty of time to play games, often betting robes, weapons – even tepees, and horses – on the outcome. At the big tribal gathering each summer, all the young men compete in archery contests, horse races, and team games like lacrosse. All year around, men play games with hoops and balls, and women play shinny, a kind of field hockey. In the winter you and your friends go tobogganing on the snowy hills and skate on frozen lakes.

There are also many games of chance. In quiet moments, hunters or warriors pass the time rolling dice into wooden bowls. In other games, each player takes a turn guessing which hand or moccasin holds a bone or specially marked stone. In the winter, the band passes the long evenings in a communal tepee listening to stories and legends told by the elders. Myths tell of heroes who kill dragons and animal spirits, like Thunderbird, whose eyes flash lightning and who makes thunder when he flaps his wings.

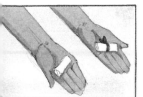

One game is played with two pieces of bone, one plain, the other marked with a string around the middle.

The guesser picks which hand the bone with the string is in. The hider shakes his fists to confuse him.

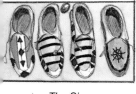

The Sioux, Omaha, and Iowa play a game with a small object such as a shiny rock and four moccasins.

One team hides the rock in one of the moccasins. The bets are laid and the other team guesses which one it is in.

Q

You have lost both your horses in a bet on a lacrosse game. How will you get some more?
Go to pages 36-37

The Indians are proud of their skills with bow and arrow. Each tribe has its own archery games. The Mandan play the Game of the Arrow.

The competitors all bring a bet – a shield, robe, or pipe – and place it on the pile. Each archer fires an arrow, then tries to get as many more in the air as he can before the first one lands. The winner may have eight or nine arrows in flight at once. He wins the whole pile of bets.

LACROSSE

Several Plains tribes, like the Choctaw, play lacrosse. The first step is to prepare the field, which is 985 feet (300 m) long with goal posts 80 feet (25 m) high.

The day before the game, the spectators place bets. Guns, pots, knives, dogs, dresses, robes, spears, go on a huge pile, and horses are tethered beside it.

There are two teams, of 300 to 350 players each! Every player has a bent stick with a webbed hoop at one end. Barefoot and wearing only loincloths, the captains meet.

Young men race the fast ponies they have bred for the hunt. At the summer camp, the proudest warriors compete, and the races are great events.

The start and finish are marked with lances. Everyone lays bets and huge crowds cheer on their relatives or favorites.

In some bands or tribes, one man is responsible for remembering the legends. Many myths involve a devious spirit like Old Man Coyote, the trickster. All the Plains tribes tell of a time when the world was a better place. People did not die, game was easy to kill, and the crow was white. Then the tricky coyote came along and made the world as it is now. The people were scared, but coyote taught them to hunt buffalo to survive.

Four medicine men, the referees, sit in the middle. Before the start, they smoke a pipe and ask the Great Spirit for good judgement and impartiality during the game.

The referees throw the ball into the air. The players chase it and try to score by throwing it between the goal posts. There are many fist-fights.

The game ends when a team scores 100, which may take all day. The winning team celebrates with triumphant dances, a feast, and all the bets they have won.

CHILDREN'S GAMES

Children copy their parents. Girls put up small tepees. A boy brings his sister a rabbit he has caught for dinner.

Boys like to play pranks on their parents. They go on mock raids, stealing meat as if they are "counting coup."

Two boys play the hoop-and-pole game. They chase a willow hoop and try to catch it on a long wooden pole.

In the winter, boys make conical tops and spin them on the ice. They also play a game like ice hockey with a leather ball.

Q

Some other boys ask you if you want to become a Kit Fox. What should you do?
Go to pages 34-35

FESTIVALS AND DANCES
HOW WOULD YOU CELEBRATE?

The double-sided drum is made from wood and stretched buffalo hide. It can be hung and played.

A BIRTH, A MARRIAGE, a successful war raid or hunt – as an Indian you will take part in dances and feasts to celebrate important events. Food and drink flow, and performers in costumes and face paint dance to the chants and driving drumbeat. Giving presents is a big part of many festivals. Rich men increase their standing by giving food or blankets to the poor.

The greatest ceremony takes place at the summer camp, when the whole tribe meets and there may be more than a thousand tepees in a giant circle on the Plain. It is time for the Sun Dance. This is a complicated ritual, and every tribe has its own ways, which have a deep religious importance and must be followed precisely. But the basic pattern is the same. The dancers, young men, stand in a circle around a pole erected at the heart of the camp. For four days, they dance and stare into the sun. They cannot eat or drink. Some men who search for a deeper faith have their chests pierced by wooden hooks tied by ropes to the pole. They dance on and on until the hooks tear through the skin and set them free. Their suffering is a gift to the Great Spirit.

The hand drum is smaller. It is played on one side with a willow drumstick wrapped in rawhide.

The water drum is a hollow log. Adding water to the reservoir at the base gives the drum a higher note.

Rattles are made from rawhide spheres (right) or gourds mounted on sticks (left). They are filled with pebbles.

Q
You would like to marry Little Wolf, but you don't know if your parents will approve. What can you do?
Go to page 16

For ceremonies or raids, men paint their faces with bright daubs of color. Some even coat their whole bodies with yellow or red clay.

Precious objects, especially painted buffalo skulls, are placed at the base of the central pole. This sacred area is called an eagle's nest or a thunderbird's nest.

DANCES

During a drought, Mandan men paint their bodies and climb a lodge to ask the sky for rain. The man who succeeds becomes known as a Rainmaker, with great spiritual powers.

Many tribes perform the Sun Dance in a lodge made of poles. This must be built in a special way. The first tree is felled by a woman chosen for her purity.

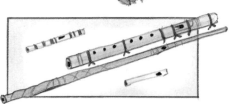

Whistles and flutes are made of wood or bones. They are played by the musicians in the Sun Dance. Young men also use them to play messages to their sweethearts.

The O-kee-pa is a Mandan Buffalo Dance. There are eight principal dancers. This one represents day and light.

Another is night and darkness who is chased away by day. Two other dancers are lifted into the air by hooks in their chests or backs.

The dance is held in spring or early summer, but not on the same date every year. For it to happen, an unhappy member of the tribe must announce that he will hold the dance to chase away his worries. Called the Pledger, he sits at the far left of the row of spectators.

His wife, the Sacred Woman, sits at the other end. A medicine man conducts the ceremony and tells the Pledger what to do. First, warriors reenact their battles. Then the dancers come out. They move by rising on their toes, often blowing wooden whistles as they gaze into the sun.

To prove that he has killed an enemy, the warrior cuts off his victim's scalp. To celebrate the raid, women sing and wave scalps on long sticks while the warriors dance.

The Mandan stage a Buffalo Dance. The dancers wear buffalo head masks and wave lances or bows. The dance goes on day and night until a herd of buffalo is found.

The Minnetaree hold a Green Corn Dance to thank the Great Spirit for the sun that ripens their crops. The dancing ends in a great corn feast for the whole tribe.

Q

Your father gives you a bag of fish and says they are for planting the corn. What is he talking about?
Go to page 25

Dog Soldiers are members of a secret society. They often police a hunt, a dance, or a move.

Councils of the whole tribe are held in a big tepee, or in the open if the tribe is on the move.

Men are respected for deeds in battle, especially counting coup – touching enemy warriors.

Men are also admired for their generosity. Great leaders give gifts to the poorer members of the band.

Q

You are out on a raid and need to start a fire. How do you do this?
Go to page 24

CHIEFS AND COUNCILS

WHO WOULD RULE YOUR BAND?

THE PLAINS TRIBES are very democratic. The chief of a band is chosen for his bravery, generosity, and wisdom. Often there are two chiefs: a war leader respected for his bravery and a peace leader known for his wisdom. A son can inherit the title of chief, but he has to earn the respect of his fellow Indians. Decisions are made at councils. All the important men are present, and they begin by smoking the pipe in silence. Then, anyone who wishes to can speak. There are no written records, so each speaker begins by summarizing the views of the last speaker, to show his respect and that he has been listening. Often the chief says very little until the end. Then he gives his decision. If all agree, the council is over; if not, it goes on. A young brave can challenge the chief's authority or call him a coward. He may be silenced, or even lead a breakaway band. Bad chiefs soon find they lead small bands!

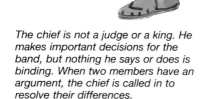

The chief is not a judge or a king. He makes important decisions for the band, but nothing he says or does is binding. When two members have an argument, the chief is called in to resolve their differences.

Red Cloud was a Oglala Sioux chief. In 1866 he led a war against soldiers who were building forts on Sioux hunting land in Montana. He won, and the Sioux burned the forts down. He died on a reservation in 1909.

Chief Joseph led the Nez Percé in a war against the U.S. army. He won one battle, crossed the Rockies, and headed for Canada. The troops caught up with him and forced him to surrender on the Plains by the border.

Sitting Bull was a Hunkpapa Sioux medicine man and leader. He was respected for his refusal to give up land to the whites. He was at the Battle of Little Bighorn, but did not fight because he was a medicine man.

SECRET SOCIETIES
Because of your reputation for bravery, some braves take you and your friend aside and ask you to join the Kit Fox Society, a secret Sioux group.

You have to buy the right to join by giving presents to an older member of the society. These include buffalo skins, a horse, some maize, and ermine furs. You work hard to get them.

You go to the society tepee to eat, talk, and dance with other members. You are now a Fox, and wear a fox-skin necklace and two eagle feathers in your hair.

Buffalo's Back Fat was head chief of the Blood Blackfoot. In 1832 he was painted by George Catlin, who wrote: "He is a dignified Indian; whilst sitting for his picture he has been surrounded by his braves . . . reciting to each other the battles they have fought."

Peace pipes

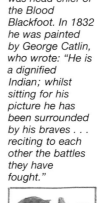

SIGN LANGUAGE

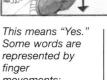

All the Plains tribes use sign language. Each action means one word or idea. This means "straight talk."

This means "Yes." Some words are represented by finger movements; others involve the whole body.

"No" is indicated by a sweeping movement of the right arm, from the chest to high above the shoulder.

"Bad" is also signaled with the right arm, this time finishing with the hand low and fingers outstretched.

Keokuk, or The Running Fox, was a leader of the Sauk. While his rival Black Hawk fought the whites, Keokuk made peace. Black Hawk was defeated and arrested, and Keokuk led the united tribe into Kansas.

Gall was an orphan who was brought up by Sitting Bull. He became war chief for Sitting Bull's Hunkpapa Sioux band, and fought alongside Crazy Horse at many battles, including the victory over Custer at Little Bighorn.

Plenty Coups was the last free-living Crow chief. He helped the U.S. army fight the Sioux, the Crow's traditional enemy. He represented all American Indians at a World War I remembrance service at Arlington, Virginia, in 1921.

You learn a song: "I am a Fox
I am supposed to die
If there is anything difficult
If there is anything dangerous
That is mine to do."

The society puts on a dance for the tribe. You wear feathers and warpaint. Four warriors paint their bodies yellow and carry lances, which are signs of their bravery.

The tribe moves camp, and the Foxes are asked to help. You make sure the women take down their tepees right away. Then you guard the rear of the convoy from enemy attack.

Q

Enemy raiders have been sighted, and the chief has decided to move camp. How is this organized?
Go to pages 18-19

The war leader White Buffalo has a vision in which he sees a Pawnee village with many horses in a valley nearby. He organizes a raid.

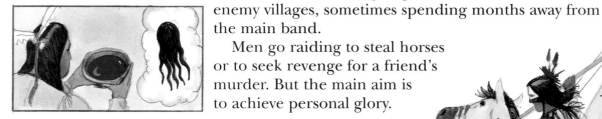

WARS AND RAIDS
WOULD YOU GO ON THE WARPATH?

ALL INDIAN MEN dream of becoming great warriors. From boyhood, they learn that bravery in battle is the greatest glory a man can achieve. Warfare between the tribes is a way of life, and every tribe has traditional enemies that it has fought for centuries. But there are no long campaigns or permanent armies. Instead, small groups of warriors lead raids on enemy villages, sometimes spending months away from the main band.

Men go raiding to steal horses or to seek revenge for a friend's murder. But the main aim is to achieve personal glory.

You stare into a bowl of buffalo blood and see a scalp. You decide to go. Your friend Two Geese sees a dog crossing his path and decides to stay.

A small group of braves paint their faces and horses in magic colors. The medicine man offers a prayer. They take food and weapons and head out.

Two scouts dressed in wolf skins go ahead on foot. They find the Pawnee village and spend the day watching it to see where the horses are tied.

The system for measuring brave deeds varies from tribe to tribe. In most tribes the greatest feat is counting coup – touching an enemy in battle. This is considered much braver than simply killing or scalping an enemy. Prisoners are rarely taken, but if they are, they are welcomed into the tribe. Men may be tortured, but children are adopted and women are married off. Warriors tell everyone about their bravery for the rest of their lives.

Q

You have killed several of the enemy. Is this because of what you ate last week?
Go to pages 20-21

The scouts find the main party by making wolf calls. They report all they have seen. They kick over a pile of buffalo dung, to show they are telling the truth.

Just before dawn the next day, you raid the village. Many horses are stolen, mostly from outside the village. You grab one superb pony tethered to a lodge.

You leap onto the fine pony and head for the meeting spot in the hills. Pawnee warriors follow, and two are killed by arrows. You grab a bow from another.

Feathers show the wearer's coups.
a Killed enemy
b Killed enemy and took scalp
c Cut enemy's throat
d Third coup
e Fifth coup
f Wounded often

Coup sticks are used to touch the enemy in battle. They are carved and decorated with feathers and fur.

A Sioux raiding party attacks a Crow camp, whooping wildly to create fear and confusion. Caught unaware, the Crow men run from their tepees and fight while the women take their children to safety. The Sioux warriors have painted their horses and shields with magical designs to protect themselves from enemy spears and arrows. The raider carrying the decorated lance is a Dog Soldier who has sworn never to turn his back on the enemy.

You ride all day and sleep in a cave that night. The next day, you stop 1 mile (2 km) from camp. Scouts send smoke signals to say that the raid was a success.

You parade around the camp showing off the stolen horses and telling everyone about your feats. The men who have taken scalps blacken their faces with charcoal.

White Buffalo has improved his standing as a visionary and war chief. He divides the booty among the raiders' families and important members of the tribe.

Q
You have fought in a great battle, and would like to record your feats on a buffalo robe. How do you do this?
Go to pages 28-29

When a boy reaches manhood, he makes a Vision Quest. He visits a sweat lodge and fasts on the Plain for days.

He has a vision in which he sees his personal guardian spirit, a red wolf. He collects objects linked to his vision.

Each object has power. The boy, now a man, wraps them in a medicine bundle to hang outside his tepee on fine days.

Opening the bundle is a sacred and elaborate ritual. The man displays each object and explains its meaning.

Q

Your mother has been sick and you decide to try and solve your problems by calling a Sun Dance. What will happen?
Go to pages 32-33

SPIRITS AND MEDICINE MEN

WHAT WOULD YOU HOPE AND FEAR?

IN THE FLIGHT OF THE EAGLE and the howl of the wolf, in every blade of grass or star in the sky, the Indians see the work of spirits. They call these spirits Powers or, sometimes, Thunders. There are many Powers, in the sun, the moon, the earth, the sky, and in every animal and plant on the Plains. Some tribes believe in one chief Power. The Sioux calling it Wankan-Tanka, meaning Great Spirit or Great Mystery. People listen carefully to the Powers and follow their advice, especially when they speak through dreams or visions. Only a

A medicine man sings and shakes his rattle to drive away the evil spirits that have made a man sick. He may change the man's name, to confuse the spirit into leaving his body. Medicine men are also excellent botanists who make ointments and potions from herbs and berries. Some contain drugs now used by modern doctors.

A DEATH IN THE FAMILY

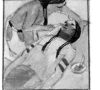

A Plains Cree man dies. The corpse is painted and dressed in his best clothes.

The legs are bound together and the hands are folded over the chest.

The corpse leaves the tepee through a hole cut in the side, not by the entrance.

A lock of hair is cut off and placed in the family's sacred bundle.

The corpse is buried with a pipe and a pot of grease. Mourners scream and cry.

Relatives gash their legs and wear rags until a chief says the mourning is over.

Unlike the Cree, most Plains tribes bury their dead on a wooden platform, often in a clump of trees. Here the body can safely rot out of the reach of wild animals. Later the family will return and bury the bones in sacred ground.

To prove his power a medicine man invites the band to a meeting. Then he works wonders, often from inside a conjuring tent.

fool would ignore what the spirits say. Before you move camp or set out on a raid or hunt, you ask the Great Spirit for a sign. Certain people are known for their power. The Indians say that these people can see the spirit world and have good medicine. The whites call them medicine men or shamans.

There are many kinds of medicine men. Some cure the sick and know what plants to use for different illnesses. Others have visions that let them see into the future. The most respected medicine men use their power to give advice and lead the band.

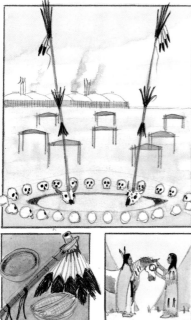

(Right) On the northwest Plains are medicine wheels. These rows of stones may have been used in sun worship or as huge calendars. Some are 3,000 years old.

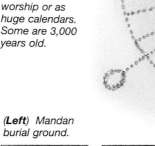

(Left) Mandan burial ground.

ARAPAHO PIPE FETISH

The Arapaho tribe believe a particular flat pipe has great spiritual power. It is kept in a special tepee.

The sacred pipe is wrapped in many layers of cloth and hung from the roof so it never touches the ground.

An Arapaho man or woman can ask the pipe for advice. He or she brings offerings of food or furs.

The Keeper of the Pipe explains how to handle it. He knows all the tribe's myths, and leads the Sun Dance. He is treated with awe.

Q
You want to make a pilgrimage to the sacred quarry where pipes are carved. How do you make one?
Go to pages 28-29

Four nights after the death, the tribe has a feast, with food and a pipe offering.

The tepee the man lived in is given away. One horse is shot; his widow gets two.

Whenever relatives pass the grave, they tend the site and hold a small feast.

CATCHING AN EAGLE

Catching eagles is a sacred activity. The hunter hides in a covered pit.

The bait is a piece of meat. He shakes this to scare off crows, wolves, or foxes.

An eagle lands. He grabs its legs, drags it into the pit, and snaps its neck.

Farmers settled on the Plains, killing game and putting up fences that stopped the roaming buffalo – and the Indians.

By 1870, hunters with high-powered rifles were killing 3 million buffalo a year. The huge herds vanished.

Hoping to strike it rich, thousands of goldpanners invaded sacred lands like the Black Hills of Dakota.

The Indians were defenseless against the white man's diseases. In 1837 smallpox killed 1675 out of 1800 Mandan.

Q

You think your chief is being cowardly and wish to challenge his leadership. How do you do this? *Go to pages 34-35*

SETTLERS AND SOLDIERS

HOW WOULD YOU DEFEND YOUR LAND?

WHITE TRADE GOODS had been reaching the Plains since the 1600s. But it was not until the mid 1800s that a great stream of pioneers, ranchers, goldpanners, and homesteaders started pouring into the "Wild West." They brought diseases that wiped out whole tribes. White hunters slaughtered millions of buffalo and farmers fenced off the open Plains. One by one, the tribes were forced off their land and onto reservations by the U.S. government. Most Indians went peacefully, but some chose to fight. They won victories, including the famous Battle of Little Bighorn. But they could never defeat the entire U.S. army. The soldiers burned their villages and hounded them without mercy. By 1890, they were all beaten, and no Plains Indian remained free.

When the American Civil War ended in 1865, many battle-hardened troops were sent to fight the Plains Indians. They were armed with big guns called Howitzers.

As Crow chief Plenty Coups said: "I see no longer the smoke rising from our lodge poles. I hear no longer the songs of the women as they prepare the meal. The antelope have gone; the buffalo wallows are empty. Only the wail of the coyote is heard. The white man's medicine is stronger than ours. . . We are like birds with a broken wing. My heart is cold within me."

To link the new state of California with the east coast, railroads were built across the Plains. The Indians tore up the track or attacked the Iron Horse (train).

Red Cloud won a victory in 1866-8. He refused to sign a peace treaty until the Sioux had razed several army forts. The whites broke the treaty immediately.

The soldiers used tactics that the Indians had never faced before. One was fighting in winter, when the tribes were normally at peace.

The first white men on the Plains were fur trappers. They usually got on well with the Indians, trading with them and adopting their ways. They brought their furs to trading posts like Fort Laramie, Wyoming, on the Oregon Trail. Such places thrived with trappers, miners, Indians, and pioneers on their way west. Later, during the Indian Wars, the U.S. army built military forts all over the West. Fort Laramie became a military complex.

The Indians had never drunk alcohol before. Many lives were ruined by the white man's "fire water."

Dull Knife left a crowded reservation and led his band of Cheyenne on a dash north. Some 60 died in the winter snows.

In 1864, soldiers attacked a Cheyenne camp at Sand Creek. At least 69 Indians, mostly women and children, died.

Whites and Indians met regularly. Chiefs went to Washington to meet the Great White Father (the U.S. president).

The Indians avoided open battles, using clever hit-and-run tactics instead. They often laid ambushes. Warriors would hide in a high spot. Then a small force would lead the soldiers into the trap. Sometimes it worked but usually the soldiers used their big guns to repel the final attack.

General Custer attacked Sitting Bull's huge camp at Little Bighorn in 1876. Led by Gall and Crazy Horse, the Indians killed all 265 soldiers, Custer included.

A new religion swept the defeated Indians in 1890. Many believed that doing the Ghost Dance would make the buffalo return and the white man vanish.

The Ghost Dance Movement ended in tragedy when soldiers massacred Big Foot's band at Wounded Knee. The chief and about 200 Sioux were killed.

Q Your brother has been killed in a fight with soldiers. How should you bury him?
Go to pages 38-39

Pictograms are an excellent source of information. Most tell the story of one warrior. But many families or bands also recorded their history or legends on buffalo hide robes, updating them regularly.

HOW DO WE KNOW?

FOR YEARS, Plains Indians were shown in films and books as bloodthirsty savages. Slowly, this image is changing, as people learn the truth about Indian ways. Barely a hundred years ago, Indians were still hunting buffalo and living freely on the Great Plains. So the best source of information is the people themselves. The Plains tribes had no written language, so many things were forgotten, especially in the desperate times after the Indian Wars. But some survivors learned English and wrote their stories down, or told them to others who had them published. Even today, there are a few men and women who grew up on reservations with elders who had lived the free life.

Many beautiful artifacts have survived in museums. So have the paintings and writings of white explorers. Warriors drew pictograms of battles they had fought in. Early photographs and government reports record the many meetings between chiefs and officials.

Some of the best accounts come from 19th-century explorers. Paul Kane painted detailed pictures of buffalo hunts on the Canadian plains in the 1840s. The American artist George Catlin spent six years recording the ways of every tribe he could visit. This picture shows him painting the portrait of the Sauk chief Keokuk, or the Running Fox.

After their defeat, Indians were forced to follow "the white man's road." Children were sent to schools where they had to wear European clothes and speak English. But recently many Indians have rediscovered their traditions, learning the old myths and craft skills such as beadwork. To do this they have often had to study artifacts like this eagle feather headdress.

Archaeologists have learned a lot about the early history of the Plains by studying grave sites and buffalo jumps. But many tribes object to white men digging up their ancestors' bones.

Some of the most beautiful records of Indian life were taken by frontier photographers like Edward Curtis. This is Walter McClintlock in a Blackfoot village in Montana.

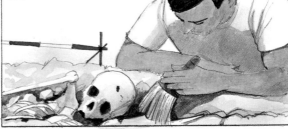

Survivors of the wars told their stories. A classic is Black Elk Speaks, the memories of a Sioux who was 13 years old at the Battle of Little Bighorn.

There are now one and a half million people with Indian heritage in the United States, and a million more in Canada. In the last thirty years, they have rediscovered their history and their pride.

This young Sioux boy is dancing at a powwow (tribal gathering) in Oklahoma.

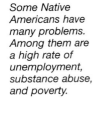

Some Native Americans have many problems. Among them are a high rate of unemployment, substance abuse, and poverty.

So is it possible to be an Indian in the age of computers? Many Indians are returning to the old traditions that respected the earth and its creatures and valued generosity, not possessions.

Banned for many years, most Plains tribes are now staging a Sun Dance every summer. Events like these help young Indians to learn the old ways.

TIMESPAN

The early history of the Plains is not very clear. Archaeological evidence shows that people were hunting buffalo and mammoths there 12,000 years ago. The freewheeling horse and gun culture began in the early 1700s. The history of the different tribes and their wars and movements is very complicated. They all have their own stories explaining where they came from.

c.1700 The Shoshone people from the west acquire horses and spread across the Plains.

c.1750 Pushed west by the Chippewa, the Sioux arrive on the Plains. They soon acquire horses and guns and become the single greatest Plains tribe.

c.1760 The Comanche get guns from the French and begin to rule the southern Plains.

1803 The United States buys a huge chunk of the West from France in the Louisiana Purchase.

1834–37 George Catlin travels among the Plains tribes, recording their ways and painting portraits of many chiefs.

1834 The important fur trading post Fort Laramie is founded on the North Platte River in Wyoming. Bands of Cheyenne, Arapaho, and Sioux begin to trade there.

1848 Gold is discovered in California. Settlers in wagon trains begin to pour into the Plains on their way west.

1851 The U.S. Congress holds a Treaty Council with Plains Indians near Fort Laramie.

1864 U.S. soldiers massacre a Cheyenne village at Sand Creek, Colorado.

1866–68 Red Cloud's War. The Oglala Sioux chief leads a huge force against soldiers building a string of forts in the Powder River country of Wyoming. The army signs a peace treaty.

1876 The U.S. army runs a winter and then a second summer campaign against the remaining free Plains Indians, who are all labeled "hostiles." On June 25, General George Custer attacks a huge camp of Sioux on the Little Bighorn River, Montana. The Indians, led by Sitting Bull, Crazy Horse, and Gall, kill all 265 soldiers, including Custer. This Indian victory, known as the Battle of Little Bighorn, or Custer's Last Stand, spells death for the Indians, who are now hunted ruthlessly.

1877 Sitting Bull escapes to Canada. Crazy Horse surrenders and is murdered by a guard.

1886 Geronimo surrenders in March, then changes his mind and escapes. Over 5,000 soldiers hunt his band of 38 Apaches without success, until they surrender again in August. The Apaches are sent to a reservation in distant Florida.

1890 Sitting Bull is shot dead, supposedly for resisting arrest. Two weeks later, Big Foot's band of unarmed Indians involved in the Ghost Dance Movement are attacked by soldiers; 153 are shot dead in the Massacre of Wounded Knee. The Plains War is over.

1909 Geronimo dies on a reservation in Oklahoma, 745 miles (1,200 km) from his home in Arizona.

1924 Native Americans are given U.S. citizenship.

Q1 Is the greatest feat you can achieve in battle to:

A Kill and scalp an enemy warrior?
B Touch an enemy with a stick?
C Steal an enemy's horse?

Q2 An old man wants to show you his medicine bundle. Do you:

A Run for your life?
B Punch him?
C Feel flattered?

Q3 Do you collect wild rice:

A With a partner, from a canoe?
B By digging it up with a bone hoe?
C On horseback?

Q4 Is a travois:

A A liar or a thief?
B A carrying frame?
C A small ax?

Q5 Are Dog Soldiers:

A Warriors in charge of pets?
B Members of a men's secret society?
C Your white enemies?

Q6 How many people are in each team of lacrosse?

A 5?
B 21?
C 300 to 350?

Q7 In winter do you hunt buffalo:

A With dog sleds?
B By setting traps in the snow?
C On snowshoes?

Q8 Someone wants to get past you in the tepee. Should you:

A Stand up and bow?
B Lean forward so they can pass behind you?
C Ask them to smoke the pipe first?

Q9 A man sets the prairie grass on fire. Why?

A To scare the buffalo into a trap?
B To prepare the soil for planting?
C To kill all the rattlesnakes?

Q10 Is the Sun Dance held:

A Every year, around Christmas?
B Every year, in early summer?
C Every ten years, at the summer solstice?

Q11 Your mother asks you to go out and get some camas. Is it:

A A small animal like an ermine?
B A sweetgrass that can be smoked like tobacco?
C A wildflower with edible bulbs?

To find out if you have survived as an American Indian check the answers on page 48.

GLOSSARY

ARAPAHO a Plains tribe that excelled at trading. The word means "he buys or trades" in Pawnee.

ASSINIBOIN or Stonies, a nomadic tribe from the northern Plains.

BAND a group of Indians from the same tribe that spend all year together.

BISON the correct name for a buffalo.

BLACKFOOT a tribe from the northern Plains. They probably got their name because they used to wear moccasins made of black skin.

BRAVE Indian warrior, usually still young.

BUFFALO large wild cow. Until the late 1800s, millions of buffalo roamed the Plains in huge herds.

BUFFALO CHIPS dried buffalo dung. The Indians gathered it and burned it.

CHEYENNE a warlike tribe from the central Plains, traditional allies of the Arapaho and enemies of the Sioux.

CHIPPEWA another name for the Ojibwa.

COMANCHE a warlike tribe that ruled the southern Plains and were famous for their skill as horsemen.

COUP (pronounced coo) an honor won in battle. The word means "blow" in French. To "count coup" a warrior had to touch an enemy with his hand or a special "coup stick."

CREE one of the biggest tribes in Canada, some of whom lived on the northern Plains.

CROW a nomadic tribe from the eastern Plains.

DAKOTA the correct name for the Sioux tribe, also spelled Lakota. The tribe gave its name to two states: North and South Dakota.

GREAT PLAINS a vast area of dry grassland 2,500 miles (4,000 km) long, from the Missouri River to the Rocky Mountains, and 620 miles (1,000 km) wide, from Alberta to Texas.

GREAT SPIRIT or Great Mystery, the chief god of many Plains tribes, including the Sioux. They believed that all power and knowledge came from the Great Spirit.

HIDATSA a prairie tribe that lived along the Missouri River.

KIOWA a nomadic tribe from the southern Plains. They were the only tribe north of Mexico to keep a written history, in the form of pictograms painted on buffalo hides. This was updated every six months from 1832 to 1939.

LODGE large circular dwelling made of logs dug into the ground and covered with earth. The prairie tribes all lived in earth lodges, sometimes dug out so the floor was 3 feet (1 m) underground. Several families shared each lodge, along with their dogs and horses. The Wichita tribe made lodges of grass. The word can also be used for a tepee.

MANDAN a prairie tribe from the upper Missouri River.

MEDICINE MAN Indian healer or holy man; also called a shaman.

MOCCASINS shoes or boots with no heels, made from soft leather.

NATIVE AMERICAN the name by which American Indians prefer to be known.

NEZ PERCE – a tribe from the Rocky Mountains that had close relationships with its Plains neighbors. The name means "pierced nose" in French.

NOMAD someone who has no fixed home and lives on the move.

OJIBWA (pronounced Oh-jib-way) or Chippewa, a tribe from the Great Lakes area on the edge of the Plains.

PARFLECHE a rawhide bag. The word means "envelope" in French.

PAWNEE a warlike prairie tribe, enemies of the Sioux. Their unusual religious practices included the sacrifice of captured women.

PEMMICAN the Plains Indians' staple food, a mixture of dried buffalo meat, fat, and cherries or grapes. The word comes from the Cree language.

PICTOGRAM a series of pictures that tell a story. Indian men painted pictograms of hunts, battles, or legends on buffalo robes and tepee covers.

POWERS the Indian word for gods or spirits. They believed that the sun, the moon, the sky, the earth, and every plant and animal on the Plains was possessed by sacred Power.

PRAIRIES the flat grassland east of the Great Plains.

SCALP the skin on the top of a person's head from which the hair grows. Indian warriors often cut off their victims' scalps to keep as war trophies. It is possible to scalp someone without killing them.

SIOUX the largest Plains tribe, the warlike Sioux (pronounced Soo) ruled the northern Plains. They numbered at least 25,000 in 1780, and about twice as many today. They are also known as the Dakota or Lakota.

SQUAW an Indian woman or wife.

SWEETGRASS plant of the Plains that the Indians smoked like tobacco.

TEPEE the Plains Indians' portable home, a cone-shaped skin tent that is easy to put up and take down. The word means "for living" in Sioux. Also spelled tipi.

TOMAHAWK a small fighting ax.

TRAVOIS wooden carrying frame that was loaded with goods and pulled by a dog or horse. Children or old or sick people could also travel by travois.

VISION QUEST when he reached puberty, an Indian boy went on a Vision Quest to try to find his own personal guardian spirit. In later times of trouble, a man would repeat the quest to get advice from his spirit or Power.

WICHITA a prairie tribe that lived in grass lodges in the winter and tepees in the summer.

INDEX

ANSWERS
HAVE YOU SURVIVED?

Here are the answers, with pages to turn to if you need an explanation. Count up your correct answers and find out your survival rating.

Q
1 (B) – page 36
2 (C) – page 38
3 (A) – page 25
4 (B) – page 18
5 (B) – page 34
6 (C) – page 30
7 (C) – page 21
8 (B) – page 15
9 (A) – page 20
10 (B) – page 32
11 (C) – page 25

10 – 11 Excellent! You will be highly respected by the rest of your band.
7 – 9 You have listened carefully to everything your parents taught you. Now they will let you marry whomever you want.
4 – 6 Playing around is all very well, but one day you may need to know what your parents have been trying to teach you!
0 – 3 Oh dear! You'll be lucky not to be scalped by an enemy!

ACKNOWLEDGEMENTS
The Salariya Book Co Ltd would like to thank the following people for their assistance:
Sarah Ridley
Eileen Batterberry